ABUNDANT TRUTH INTERNATIONAL MINISTRIES

C.O.G.I.C. Protocols Series

THE MANDATE OF THE EXPEDITOR

A Brief Guide to the Protocols of C.O.G.I.C. Expeditors and Masters of Ceremonies

Roderick Levi Evans

The Mandate of the Expeditor

A Brief Guide to the Protocols of C.O.G.I.C. Expeditors and Masters of Ceremonies

All Rights Reserved ©2022 Roderick L. Evans

No part of this book may be reproduced or transmitted in any form or by any means, graphic, electronic, or mechanical, including photocopying, recording, taping, or by any information storage or retrieval system, without the permission in writing from the publisher.

Abundant Truth Publishing
an imprint of Abundant Truth International Ministries

For information address:
Abundant Truth International
P.O. Box 126
Camden, NC 279

Unless otherwise indicated, all of the scripture quotations are taken from the *Authorized King James Version* **of the Bible. Scripture quotations marked with NIV are taken from the** *New International Version* **of the Bible. Scripture quotations marked with NASV are taken from the** *New American Standard Version* **of the Bible. Scripture quotations marked with Amplified are taken from the** *Amplified Bible.*

ISBN 13: 9798293925254

Printed in the United States of America

Disclaimer: The information presented is not officially endoresed by the Church or any Jurisidiction, but provided as a supplement to the established order and protocols of the C.O.G.I.C.

Contents

Introduction

Section 1 - The Purpose of the Expeditor   1

The Objective of the Expeditor   3

The Order of the Expeditor   5

Section 2 – The Ministry of the Expeditor   9

Focus   12

Facilitate   12

Fortify   013

Section 3 - The Mission of the Forerunner   19

The Ministry of the Forerunner   21

Contents (cont.)

The Purpose of the Forerunner   24

Section 4 – The Gift of Exhortation   31

The Purpose of Exhortation   33

The Practice of the Exhorter   35

Section 5 – Flowing in the Holy Spirit   39

Intrusion   41

Subjection   43

Section 6 – Protocols & Precautions   47

Giving of Honors   49

Follow the Program   50

Contents (cont.)

Section 7 – The Offering   57

The Gracious Appeal   59
The Generous Example   60
Concluding Statement   61

Contents (cont.)

Section 7 – The Offering   57

The Gracious Appeal   59
The Generous Example   60
Concluding Statement   61

Introduction

The Church of God in Christ is a church built on spiritual principles and practices. The church is known for its order and respect of its leaders.

The C.O.G.I.C. Protocols Series is developed to help those within the church execute their duties and ministries within the standards set by the church.

In this publication

In this publication, we will discuss the mandate of the expeditor and the master/mistress of ceremony in C.O.G.I.C. religious services. Protocols and procedures are given for the execution of this duty.

In addition, spiritual guidelines and practical application are provided. The information will provide clarity and instruction for those fulfilling the ministry in the church.

THE MANDATE OF THE EXPEDITOR

-Section 1-

The Purpose of the Expeditor

THE MANDATE OF THE EXPEDITOR

The voice of one crying in the wilderness, prepare ye the way of the Lord, make his paths straight. (Mark 1:3)

THE MANDATE OF THE EXPEDITOR

The overall purpose of the expeditor is to ensure proper order and decorum is maintained in the spiritual setting.

The expeditor must maintain focus and discretion, while allowing for unforeseen fluctuations in any given setting.

The Objective of the Expeditor

The expeditor prepares and leads the people into proper worship.

Go through, go through the gates; prepare ye the way of the people; cast up, cast up the highway; gather out the stones; lift up a standard for

THE MANDATE OF THE EXPEDITOR

the people. - Isaiah 62:10

A. **Expedite**: to execute promptly; to accelerate the process or progress of – Miriam Webster Dictionary.

B. **Other titles for Expeditors**: Facilitators, Master or Mistress of Ceremony, Moderators, and the Like.

C. **Prepare the Way of the People**: The expeditor makes sure the setting goes according to plan, schedule, program, or instructions in a timely, professional, and spiritual manner.

THE MANDATE OF THE EXPEDITOR

The Order of the Expeditor

Even in the scriptures, Paul gave guidelines for the operation of the gifts in the religious setting. When he concluded his admonitions, he writes,

Let all things be done decently and in order. (I Corinthians 14: 40)

In the Pentecostal worship service, there are times of exuberance and praise and the manifestations of spiritual gifts, such as tongues and prophecy. The expeditor must not be afraid to maintain order, even when these things

THE MANDATE OF THE EXPEDITOR

are in demonstration.

THE MANDATE OF THE EXPEDITOR

Service Notes:

THE MANDATE OF THE EXPEDITOR

THE MANDATE OF THE EXPEDITOR

-Section 2-

The Ministry of the Expeditor

THE MANDATE OF THE EXPEDITOR

Wherefore the rather, brethren, give diligence to make your calling and election sure: for if ye do these things, ye shall never fall: (2 Peter 1:10)

THE MANDATE OF THE EXPEDITOR

Three-Fold Purpose: Foundationally sets the tone for the Administration of the Word. The expeditor should view his or her role as the governing ministry in the setting. The expeditor ministry is always in subjection to the Pastor or organizer of the setting. The expeditor should have a threefold mission.

> *And I will bring the blind by a way that they knew not; I will lead them in paths that they have not known I will make darkness light before them, and crooked things straight. These things will I do*

THE MANDATE OF THE EXPEDITOR

unto them, and not forsake them.

- Isaiah 42: 16

Focus

The first purpose of the expeditor's role is to bring **focus** to the hearts and minds of the people by establishing the goals of the setting as the people are addressed. Oftentimes, people's attention needs to be redirected from the affairs and cares of the life to properly engage in the service at hand.

Facilitate

Second, the expeditor has to be spiritually aware to **facilitate** the move

THE MANDATE OF THE EXPEDITOR

of the Holy Spirit in a service. When gifts like speaking and tongues and prophecy are in operation, the expeditor must be able to allow these things to be done in an orderly fashion.

There will be times when the Spirit will move on the congregation with great power or lead individuals to move in some form of ministry. The expeditor must know how to administrate these things.

Fortify

Third, the expeditor must **fortify** the service against disorder and guard against spiritual attacks. In the Book of Job, we discover that when the angels gathered together, Lucifer came before God as well.

This demonstrates that even in the religious setting, the enemy will do things to bring distraction and disorders.

In the Pentecostal setting, this sometimes is demonstrated in false "moves" and manifestations masquerading as a work of the Spirit, Paul said that the devil will appear as an angel of light.

In services, the enemy can cause emotional upheavals to hinder people from receiving the word of God.

THE MANDATE OF THE EXPEDITOR

Again, when in doubt, the expeditor should look to the Pastor or the organizer of the event or service.

THE MANDATE OF THE EXPEDITOR

THE MANDATE OF THE EXPEDITOR

Service Notes:

_____

_____

_____

_____

_____

_____

_____

_____

THE MANDATE OF THE EXPEDITOR

THE MANDATE OF THE EXPEDITOR

-Section 3-

The Mission of the Forerunner

THE MANDATE OF THE EXPEDITOR

And he shall go before him in the spirit and power of Elias, to turn the hearts of the fathers to the children, and the disobedient to the wisdom of the just; to make ready a people prepared for the Lord. (Luke 1:17)

THE MANDATE OF THE EXPEDITOR

The expeditor serves the service as John did the coming of Christ. The expeditor foundationally sets the tone for the Administration of the Word.

The expeditor should view his or her role as the governing ministry in the setting. The expeditor's ministry is always in subjection to the Pastor or organizer of the setting. The expeditor should have a threefold mission.

The Ministry of the Forerunner

The expeditor's role parallels the ministry of John the Baptist.

The voice of him that crieth in the

THE MANDATE OF THE EXPEDITOR

wilderness, Prepare ye the way of the LORD, make straight in the desert a highway for our God. Isaiah 40:3

A. John prepared the people for the coming of the Lord. - *The voice of one crying in the wilderness, Prepare ye the way of the Lord, make his paths straight. (Mark 1:3)*

B. John had a clear, concise, prophetic message. – *In those days came John the Baptist, preaching in the wilderness of Judaea, And saying, Repent ye: for*

THE MANDATE OF THE EXPEDITOR

the kingdom of heaven is at hand. Matthew 3:1-2

C. John understood his place – *I am not the one" – And they asked him, What then? Art thou Elias? And he saith, I am not. Art thou that prophet? And he answered, No. 22Then said they unto him, who art thou? that we may give an answer to them that sent us. What sayest thou of thyself? 23He said, I am the voice of one crying in the wilderness, Make straight the way of the Lord, as said the prophet*

THE MANDATE OF THE EXPEDITOR

Esaias. John 1:21-23

D. John exercised spiritual discernment – *The next day John seeth Jesus coming unto him, and saith, Behold the Lamb of God, which taketh away the sin of the world. John 1:29*

E. John understood when it was time for him to decrease and move off the scene – *He must increase, but I must decrease. John 3:30*

The Purpose of the Forerunner

It is then established that John's ministry is a prime example of the

THE MANDATE OF THE EXPEDITOR

expeditor's role. John knew that his ministry was **preparatory** for the coming of the Messiah. The expeditor must know that how they facilitate should prepare the people for the ministry of the Word.

Whatever exhortations and directives they give as they expedite the service should prepare the hearts and minds of the people to receive the engrafted word of God.

John had one message which was to call the people to repentance. Likewise, the expeditor has one "message" which to exhort the people to worship God and

THE MANDATE OF THE EXPEDITOR

receive the coming message and messenger.

John understood that he was not the Messiah. The expeditor should know that they are not in place to preach and teach, but to prepare the people to receive the designated messenger.

John exercised discernment to know which people were truly repentant as opposed to those who genuinely wanted his ministry. The expeditor has to know what things are necessary and unnecessary in the religious setting.

Finally, John understood that his

THE MANDATE OF THE EXPEDITOR

ministry was limited and that it was coming to its conclusion.

He must increase, but I must decrease. (John 3:30)

The expeditor must know that their involvement in the service is limited and should know when to bring the service in order to receive the word of God.

THE MANDATE OF THE EXPEDITOR

THE MANDATE OF THE EXPEDITOR

Service Notes:

_____

_____

_____

_____

_____

_____

_____

_____

_____

THE MANDATE OF THE EXPEDITOR

THE MANDATE OF THE EXPEDITOR

-Section 4-

The Gift of Exhortation

THE MANDATE OF THE EXPEDITOR

Having then gifts differing according to the grace that is given to us, whether prophecy, let us prophesy according to the proportion of faith; Or ministry, let us wait on our ministering: or he that teacheth, on teaching; Or he that exhorteth, on exhortation: he that giveth, let him do it with simplicity; he that ruleth, with diligence; he that sheweth mercy, with cheerfulness.
(Romans 12:6-8)

THE MANDATE OF THE EXPEDITOR

The expeditor must pray for the **ministry gift of exhortation**. It is listed among the spiritual gifts. Believers are exhorted to desire spiritual gits, exhortation being among them.

The Purpose of Exhortation

The Expeditor must view his or her task as a *forerunner* through the execution of the gift of exhortation.

> *Having then gifts differing according to the grace that is given to us, whether prophecy, let us prophesy according to the proportion of faith; Or ministry, let*

THE MANDATE OF THE EXPEDITOR

us wait on our ministering: or he that teacheth, on teaching; Or he that exhorteth, on **exhortation**. *– I Corinthians 12:7-8*

The expeditor must remember that exhortation should not be confused with preaching. The statements of the exhortatory are always a call-to-action within the service, culminating with the directive to receive the main sermon or message.

If the function does not culminate with preaching, then the expeditor must move the service towards the main or

THE MANDATE OF THE EXPEDITOR

featured presentation(s).

The Practice of the Exhorter

    A. The expeditor prepares the setting for effectual, spiritual worship.

    B. The expeditor exhorts, encourages, and challenges those gathered to enter into worship.

    C. The expeditor understands their role, position, and purpose as the forerunner to the primary messenger.

        The expeditor should not set out to be the primary preacher or miracle and deliverance ministry.

THE MANDATE OF THE EXPEDITOR

D. The expeditor should have spiritual discernment to facilitate and protect the sanctity of the service.

E. The expeditor must be disciplined to know how to move in and out of the way so that the service goes uninterrupted or influenced by personal motives and agendas. – John 3:30

THE MANDATE OF THE EXPEDITOR

Service Notes:

_____

_____

_____

_____

_____

_____

_____

_____

C.O.G.I.C. Protocols Series

THE MANDATE OF THE EXPEDITOR

-Section 5-

Flowing in the Holy Spirit

For as many as are led by the Spirit of God, they are the sons of God.
(Romans 8:14)

THE MANDATE OF THE EXPEDITOR

The ministry of exhortation must take precedence over any other gifts the expeditor may have. The expeditor must know how to how to flow between personal spiritual endowments and maintaining order in the service.

Intrusion

The expeditor who has other ministries within him/her should know how to maintain discipline. The temptation to move in other giftings and ministries can be great. Remember, when Paul gave the directives for facilitating prophecy.

He said that there should be no more

than three dominant prophecies given. He then states that if another prophet has a word, they should remain silent, because the prophet does not have to release that word because its release is in subjection to the prophet.

And the spirits of the prophets are subject to the prophets. (I Corinthians 14:32)

The expeditor who has a preaching ministry has to be careful not to move into their ministry of preaching. They cannot **intrude** into other areas of ministry not mandated for them by the host. The

THE MANDATE OF THE EXPEDITOR

expeditor simply has to exercise control.

Subjection

The expeditor that has a preaching or teaching ministry must not operate in this ministry while they are facilitating the service. They must allow exhortation to come forth and not preaching, teaching, or instruction. Those things are reserved for the messenger of the service or event. They may receive revelation, but it is not for them to share.

The expeditor has to know who to use other gifts under subjection to the ministry of exhortation to keep service

THE MANDATE OF THE EXPEDITOR

moving and not change its tone or direction.

`There are times when it will be appropriate for the expeditor to move in other giftings. However, the expeditor must be in subject to the Pastor or the event organizer and then follow the unction of the Holy Spirit. The expeditor should operate in those gifts, but do not position themselves as the main speaker or presenter.

THE MANDATE OF THE EXPEDITOR

Service Notes:

_____

_____

_____

_____

_____

_____

_____

_____

THE MANDATE OF THE EXPEDITOR

-Section 6-

Protocols & Precautions

THE MANDATE OF THE EXPEDITOR

But let all things be done decently, and according to order. (I Corinthians 14:40)

THE MANDATE OF THE EXPEDITOR

Giving of Honors (Protocol/Precaution 1)

Regardless of the type of service, it is always in order to address the house. Standard procedure is that when the service opens, honor is to be given to all whom honor is due: from the highest ranking official and then so on.

Render therefore to all their dues: tribute to whom tribute is due; custom to whom custom; fear to whom fear; honour to whom honour. - Romans 13:7

After the house has been addressed,

THE MANDATE OF THE EXPEDITOR

admonish those on the program to not repeat addressing the whole house.

The simple statement of "the house has already been addressed" should be given as a guideline.

This helps the service to move expeditiously. Never forget to give honor to one's own Pastor, whether they are present or not.

**Follow the Program
(Protocol/Precaution 2)**

When in doubt of what to do, always follow the program or instructions already

THE MANDATE OF THE EXPEDITOR

given.

A. Open with a brief welcome and invitation to enter into worship (Use a quote from a psalm or hymn).

Within COGIC, use the manual as a guideline as to what scriptures are appropriate for the differing services.

B. Fortify parts of the service as needed with brief exhortations – Always have a smile and upbeat demeanor.

Do not berate the people, but consistently encourage them to praise God and remember His works in their lives.

THE MANDATE OF THE EXPEDITOR

C. Establish communication and/or eye contact with those in charge in case of any changes.

When possible, establish non-verbal signals with the Pastor or event organizer as the service progresses. This will ensure that order and clarity for the service will be maintained.

D. Make way for the move of the Spirit as appropriate – be aware of time constraints, instructions from leader, and soulish/emotional worship.

The expeditor must make way for the

move of the Holy Spirit. However, they must keep the service moving in a godly, timely, and orderly manner.

E. If someone is out of order or an unforeseen change is made, handle with discretion, care, and respect in the fear of Lord.

If someone is unruly or "out of order," discreetly ask an usher, deacon, or armor-bearer for help. Do not address the individual from the platform but allow those in place to handle them.

THE MANDATE OF THE EXPEDITOR

This will minimize the distraction, and the service will proceed with minimal disturbance or interference.

THE MANDATE OF THE EXPEDITOR

Service Notes:

THE MANDATE OF THE EXPEDITOR

THE MANDATE OF THE EXPEDITOR

-Section 7-

The Offering

THE MANDATE OF THE EXPEDITOR

You must each decide in your heart how much to give. And do not give reluctantly or in response to pressure. For God loves a person who gives cheerfully. (2 Corinthians 9:7)

THE MANDATE OF THE EXPEDITOR

Remember, receiving offering is a spiritual heritage of the Church. It is designed to further the work of the Lord, support its servants, and bless those who are in need.

The Gracious Appeal

A. Make the appeal with a brief anecdote, testimony, or scripture. Remind the people of the blessings of tithes, offering, and giving.

B. Always have a smile and general cheer as you admonish the people.

THE MANDATE OF THE EXPEDITOR

Paul admonished the people to give cheerfully. The proper attitude will always incur the favor of God.

C. Do not talk of your personal financial situation or difficulties (unless it is a testimony of provision) but demonstrate goodwill.

The Generous Example

A. Ask for the amount given via instructions, if no amount is given, follow the general guidelines for the setting, but always ask the people to give liberally.

THE MANDATE OF THE EXPEDITOR

B. If known before hand, especially for special offerings, try to have the requested amount so that you can serve as an example to those who are giving.

C. If you do have the requested goal to give, let it be known as a visible means to encourage others.

D. If you do not have the set giving goal, **this does not have to be made known**, yet admonish those who can and will.

Concluding Statement

The expeditor is an important part to

any service. This role should be performed in such a way that God is glorified, order is maintained, and the people are blessed.

THE MANDATE OF THE EXPEDITOR

Service Notes:

_____

_____

_____

_____

_____

_____

_____

_____

_____

THE MANDATE OF THE EXPEDITOR

THE MANDATE OF THE EXPEDITOR

Service Notes:

_____

_____

_____

_____

_____

_____

_____

_____

THE MANDATE OF THE EXPEDITOR